Time's Power

W · W · NORTON & COMPANY | *NEW YORK · LONDON*

Adrienne Rich

POEMS 1985–1988

Time's Power

Thanks to the following magazines in which some of these poems first appeared: *American Poetry Review*; *Field*; *Jewish Currents*; *Lilith*; *Poetry* (Seventy-fifth Anniversary issue); *Sequoia*; *Sinister Wisdom*; *Tri-Quarterly*, a publication of Northwestern University; *The Woman's Review of Books*; *Yale Review*.

Published simultaneously in Canada by Penguin Books Canada Ltd, 2801 John Street, Markham, Ontario L3R 1B4
Printed in the United States of America.

The text of this book is composed in 11/13 Garamond No. 3,
with display type set in Centaur.
Composition by PennSet, Inc.
Manufacturing by The Haddon Craftsmen, Inc.
Book design by Antonina Krass.

First Edition

Library of Congress Cataloging-in-Publication Data
Rich, Adrienne Cecile.
Time's power: poems 1985–1988 / Adrienne Rich.—1st ed.
p.   cm.
I. Title.
PS3535.I233T5   1989
811'.54—dc19   88-29059

ISBN 0-393-02677-9

ISBN 0-393-30575-9 PBK.

W. W. Norton & Company, Inc., 500 Fifth Avenue, New York, N.Y. 10110
W. W. Norton & Company Ltd., 37 Great Russell Street, London WC1B 3NU

1 2 3 4 5 6 7 8 9 0

For Michelle

CONTENTS

Time's Power

SOLFEGGIETTO

1.

Your windfall at fifteen   your Steinway grand
paid for by fire insurance
came to me as birthright   a black cave
with teeth of ebony and ivory
twanging and thundering over the head
of the crawling child   until
that child was set on the big book on the chair
to face the keyboard world of black and white
—already knowing the world was black and white
The child's hands   smaller than a sand-dollar
set on the keys   wired to their mysteries
the child's wits facing the ruled and ruling staves

2.

For years we battled over music lessons
mine, taught by you   Nor did I wonder
what that keyboard meant to you
the hours of solitude   the practising
your life of prize-recitals   lifted hopes
Piatti's nephew praising you at sixteen
scholarships to the North
Or what it was to teach
boarding-school girls what won't be used
shelving ambition   beating time
to "On the Ice at Sweet Briar" or
"The Sunken Cathedral" for a child
counting the minutes and the scales to freedom

3.
Freedom: what could that mean, for you or me?
—Summers of '36, '37, Europe untuned
what I remember isn't lessons
not Bach or Brahms or Mozart
but the rented upright in the summer rental
One Hundred Best-Loved Songs on the piano rack
And so you played, evenings   and so we sang
"Steal Away" and "Swanee River,"
"Swing Low," and most of all
"Mine Eyes Have Seen the Glory of the Coming of the Lord"
How we sang out the chorus   how I loved
the watchfires of the hundred circling camps
and *truth is marching on* and *let us die to make men free*

4.
Piano lessons   The mother and the daughter
Their doomed exhaustion   their common mystery
worked out in finger-exercises   Czerny, Hanon
The yellow Schirmer albums   quarter-rests   double-holds
glyphs of an astronomy   the mother cannot teach
the daughter because this is not the story
of a mother teaching magic to her daughter
Side by side I see us locked
My wrists   your voice   are tightened
Passion lives in old songs   in the kitchen
where another woman cooks   teaches   and sings
He shall feed his flock like a shepherd
and in the booklined room
where the Jewish father reads and smokes and teaches
Ecclesiastes, Proverbs, the Song of Songs
The daughter struggles with the strange notations
—dark chart of music's ocean   flowers and flags
but would rather learn by ear and heart   The mother
says she must learn to read by sight   not ear and heart

5.

Daughter who fought her mother's lessons—
even today a scrip of music balks me—
I feel illiterate in this
your mother-tongue   Had it been Greek or Slovak
no more could your native alphabet have baffled
your daughter   whom you taught for years
held by a tether   over the ivory
and ebony teeth of the Steinway
                                        It is
the three hundredth anniversary of Johann
Sebastian Bach   My earliest life
woke to his English Suites   under your fingers
I understand a language I can't read
Music you played streams on the car radio
in the freeway night
You kept your passions deep   You have them still
I ask you, both of us
—Did you think mine was a virtuoso's hand?
Did I see power in yours?
What was worth fighting for?   What did you want?
What did I want from you?

1985–1988

♀ *THIS*

Face flashing free   child-arms
lifting the collie pup
torn paper on the path
Central Park   April '72
behind you   minimal
those benches and that shade
that brilliant light in which
you laughed longhaired
and I'm the keeper of
this little piece of paper
this little piece of truth

I wanted this from you—
laughter   a child turning
into a boy   at ease
in the spring light   with friends
I wanted this for you

I could mutter   *Give back*
that day   give me again
that child   with the chance
of making it all right
I could yell   *Give back that light*
on the dog's teeth   the child's hair
but no rough drafts are granted
—Do you think I don't remember?
did you think I was all-powerful
unimpaired   unappalled?
yes   you needed that from me
I wanted this from you

1985

6

ꝃ LOVE POEM

Tell me, bristler, where
do you get such hair
so quick a flare   so strong a tongue

Green eyes   fierce curls
there and here a mole
a girl's
dimples   a warrior's mind

dark blood under gold skin
testing, testing the world
the word

and so to write for you
a pretty sonnet
would be untrue

to your mud-river flashing
over rocks   your delicate
coffee-bushes

and more I cannot know
and some I labor with
and I mean to stay true

even in poems, to you
But there's something more

Beauty, when you were young
we both thought we were young
now that's all done

we're serious now
about death   we talk to her
daily, as to a neighbor

we're learning to be true
with her   she has the keys
to this house   if she must

she can sleep over

1986

NEGOTIATIONS

Someday if someday comes we will agree
that trust is not about safety
that keeping faith is not about deciding
to clip our fingernails exactly
to the same length or wearing
a uniform that boasts our unanimity

Someday if someday comes we'll know
the difference between liberal laissez-faire
pluralism and the way you cut your hair
and the way I clench my hand
against my cheekbone
both being possible gestures of defiance

Someday if there's a someday we will
bring food, you'll say I can't eat what you've brought
I'll say Have some in the name of our
trying to be friends, you'll say What about you?
We'll taste strange meat and we'll admit
we've tasted stranger

Someday if someday ever comes we'll go
back and reread those poems and manifestos
that so enraged us in each other's hand
I'll say, But damn, you wrote it so I
couldn't write it off   You'll say
I read you always, even when I hated you

1986

9

IN A CLASSROOM

Talking of poetry, hauling the books
arm-full to the table where the heads
bend or gaze upward, listening, reading aloud,
talking of consonants, elision,
caught in the how, oblivious of why:
I look in your face, Jude,
neither frowning nor nodding,
opaque in the slant of dust-motes over the table:
a presence like a stone, if a stone were thinking
What I cannot say, is me. For that I came.

1986

THE NOVEL

All winter you went to bed early, drugging yourself on *War and
     Peace*
Prince Andrei's cold eyes taking in the sky from the battlefield
were your eyes, you went walking wrapped in his wound
like a padded coat against the winds from the two rivers
You went walking in the streets as if you were ordinary
as if you hadn't been pulling with your raw mittened hand
on the slight strand that held your tattered mind
blown like an old stocking from a wire
on the wind between two rivers.
                              All winter you asked nothing
of that book though it lay heavy on your knees
you asked only for a shed skin, many skins in which to walk
you were old woman, child, commander
you watched Natasha grow into a neutered thing
you felt your heart go still while your eyes swept the pages
you felt the pages thickening to the left and on the right-
hand growing few, you knew the end was coming
you knew beyond the ending lay
your own, unwritten life

1986

P A STORY

Absence is homesick. Absence wants a home.
but Absence left without a glance at Home.
Home tried to hold in Absence's despite,
Home caved, shuddered, yet held
without Absence's consent. Home took a walk
in several parks, Home shivered
in outlying boroughs, slept on strange floors,
cried many riffs of music, many words.
Home went out to teach school, Home studied pain control
Home learned to dive and came up blind with blood
Home learned to live on each location
but whenever Absence called, Home had to answer
in the grammar of Absence.
                                Home would hitch-hike
through flying snow, Home would roast meat,
light candles, to withstand the cold. Home washed the dishes
faithfully. But Absence
always knew when to call.
                              What if Absence calls
and a voice answers
                        in the accent of Home?

1986

IN MEMORIAM: D.K.

A man walking on the street
feels unwell   has felt unwell
all week, a little   Yet the flowers crammed
in pots on the corner: furled anemones:
he knows they open
burgundy, violet, pink, amarillo
all the way to their velvet cores
The flowers hanging over the fence: fuchsias:
each tongued, staring,   all of a fire:
the flowers   He who has
been happy oftener than sad
carelessly happy   well oftener than sick
one of the lucky   is thinking about death
and its music   about poetry
its translations of his life

And what good will it do you
to go home and put on the Mozart Requiem?
Read Keats?   How will culture cure you?

Poor, unhappy

unwell culture   what can it sing or say
six weeks from now, to you?

Give me your living hand   If I could take the hour
death moved into you   undeclared, unnamed
—even if sweet, if I could take that hour

between my forceps   tear at it like a monster
wrench it out of your flesh   dissolve its shape in quicklime
and make you well again
                              no, not again
but still. . . .

1986

CHILDREN PLAYING CHECKERS
AT THE EDGE OF THE FOREST

Two green-webbed chairs
                              a three-legged stool between
Your tripod
                  Spears of grass
                                    longer than your bare legs
cast shadows on your legs
                              drawn up
                                          from the red-and-black
cardboard squares
                        the board of play
                                    the board of rules
But you're not playing, you're talking
                                    It's midsummer
and greater rules are breaking
                                    It's the last
innocent summer you will know
                                    and I
will go on awhile pretending that's not true

When I have done pretending
                              I can see this:
the depth of the background
                        shadows
                                    not of one moment only
erased and charcoaled in again
                              year after year

how the tree looms back behind you
the first tree of the forest
                              the last tree
from which the deer step out
                          from protection
                                        the first tree
into dreadfulness
                  The last and the first tree

1987

SLEEPWALKING NEXT TO DEATH

Sleep   horns of a snail
                    protruding, retracting
What we choose to know
                    or not know
                              all these years
sleepwalking
          next to death

                              I

This snail could have been eaten
This snail could have been crushed
This snail could have dreamed it was a painter or a poet
This snail could have driven fast at night
putting up graffiti with a spray-gun:

This snail could have ridden
in the back of the pick-up, handing guns

                              II

Knows, chooses not to know
                    It has always
been about death and chances
                    The Dutch artist wrote and painted
one or more strange and usable things
For I mean to meet you
in any land   in any language
This is my promise:
I will be there
if you are there

III

In between this and that there are different places
of waiting, airports mostly where the air
is hungover, visibility low   boarding passes not guaranteed
If you wrote me, *I sat next to Naomi*
I would read that, *someone who felt like Ruth*
I would begin reading you like a dream
That's how extreme it feels

                              that's what I have to do

IV

Every stone around your neck you know the reason for
at this time in your life   Relentlessly
you tell me their names and furiously I
forget their names   Forgetting the names of the stones
you love, you lover of stones
what is it I do?

V

What is it I do? I refuse to take your place
in the world   I refuse to make myself
your courier   I refuse so much
I might ask, what is it I do?
I will not be the dreamer for whom
you are the only dream
I will not be your channel
I will wrestle you to the end
for our difference (as you have wrestled me)
I will change your name and confuse
the Angel

VI

I am stupid with you and practical with you
I remind you to take a poultice   forget a quarrel
I am a snail in the back of the pick-up handing you
vitamins you hate to take

VII

Calmly you look over my shoulder   at this page   and say
It's all about you   None of this
tells my story

VIII

Yesterday noon I stood by a river
and many waited to cross over
from the Juarez barrio
                    to El Paso del Norte
First day of spring   a stand of trees
in Mexico were in palegreen leaf
a man casting a net
                    into the Rio Grande
and women, in pairs, strolling
                        across the border
as if taking a simple walk
                    Many thousands go

I stood by the river and thought of you
young   in Mexico   in a time of hope

IX

The practical nurse is the only nurse
with her plastic valise of poultices and salves
her hands of glove leather and ebony
her ledgers of pain
The practical nurse goes down to the river
in her runover shoes and her dollar necklace
eating a burrito in hand
                          it will be a long day
a long labor
                  the midwife will be glad to see her
it will be a long night   someone bleeding
from a botched abortion   a beating   Will you let her touch you
                          now?
Will you tell her you're fine?

X

I'm afraid of the border patrol
                          Not those men
of La Migra who could have run us
into the irrigation canal with their van
                              I'm afraid
of the patrollers
the sleepwalker in me
                          the loner in you

I want five hours with you
in a train running south
                    maybe ten hours
in a Greyhound bound for the border
the two seats side-by-side that become a home
an island of light in the continental dark
the time that takes the place of a lifetime
I promise I won't fall asleep when the lights go down
I will not be lulled
Promise you won't jump the train
vanish into the bus depot at three a.m.
that you won't defect
                    that we'll travel
like two snails
                our four horns erect

1987

⊬LETTERS IN THE FAMILY

I: Catalonia 1936

Dear Parents:
                    I'm the daughter
you didn't bless when she left,
an unmarried woman wearing a khaki knapsack
with a poor mark in Spanish.
                                    I'm writing now
from a plaster-dusted desk in a town
pocked street by street with hand grenades,
some of them, dear ones, thrown by me.
This is a school: the children are at war.
You don't need honors in schoolroom Spanish here
to be of use and my right arm
's as strong as anyone's. I sometimes think
all languages are spoken here,
even mine, which you got zero in.
Don't worry. Don't try to write. I'm happy,
if you could know it.
                                    Rochelle.

II: Yugoslavia, 1944

Dear Chana,
                    where are you now?
Am sending this pocket-to-pocket
(though we both know pockets we'd hate to lie in).
They showed me that poem you gave Reuven,
about the match:
Chana, you know, I never was
for martyrdom. I thought we'd try our best,
ragtag mission that we were,

then clear out if the signals looked too bad.
Something in you drives things ahead for me
but if I can I mean to stay alive.
We're none of us giants, you know,
just small, frail, inexperienced romantic people.
But there are things we learn.
You know the sudden suck of empty space
between the jump and the ripcord pull?
I hate it. I hate it so,
I've hated you for your dropping
ecstatically in free-fall, in the training,
your look, dragged on the ground, of knowing
precisely why you were there.
                                                  My mother's
still in Palestine. And yours
still there in Hungary. Well, there we are.
When this is over—
                              I'm
your earthbound friend to the end, still yours—

                                                            Esther.

III: Southern Africa, 1986

Dear children:
                        We've been walking nights
a long time over rough terrain,
sometimes through marshes. Days we hide
under what bushes we can find.
Our stars steer us. I write
on my knee by a river with a weary hand,
and the weariness will come through
this letter that should tell you
nothing but love. I can't say where we are,
what weeds are in bloom, what birds cry at dawn.
The less you know the safer.

But not to know how you are going on—
Matile's earache, Emma's lessons, those tell-tale
eyes and tongues, so quick—are you remembering
to be brave and wise and strong?
At the end of this hard road
we'll sit all together at one meal
and I'll tell you everything: the names
of our comrades, how the letters
were routed to you, why I left.
And I'll stop and say, "Now you,
grown so big, how was it for you, those times?
Look, I know you in detail, every inch of each
sweet body, haven't I washed and dried you
a thousand times?"
                    And we'll eat and tell our stories
together. That is my reason.
                                        Ma.

1987

THE DESERT AS GARDEN OF PARADISE

1.

Guard the knowledge
from the knowledgeable,
those who gobble:
make it unpalatable.

Stars in this place
might look
distant to me as you,
to you as me.

Monotheism. Where it began.
But all the spirits, too.
Desert says: What you believe
I can prove. I: amaranth flower,
I: metamorphic rock, I: burrow,
I: water-drop in tilted catchment,
I: vulture, I: driest thorn.

Rocks in a trance. Escaped
from the arms of other rocks.
Roads leading to gold and to false gold.

2.

I ask you to sing, Chavela, in the desert
on tapes pirated from smuggled LP's
I bring you here with me: I ask you to sing

It's not for me, your snarling contralto
caught on a backdrop of bitter guitar
not for me   yet I pray let me listen

I don't pray often   Never to male or female
sometimes to music or the flask of sunset
quick winter evenings   draining into the ground

our blood is mixed in, borderland magenta
and vermilion, never to become one
yet what we're singing, dying in, that color

two-worlded, never one   Where from bars
lit by candle and earthquake your music finds me
whom it didn't look for   This is why I ask you,

when the singing escapes the listener and goes
from the throat to where the mountains hang in chains
as if they never listened   why the song

wants so much to go where no song has ever gone.

3.
In this pale clear light where all mistakes are bathed
this afterglow of westernness
I write to you, head wrapped in your darkred scarf

framed by the sharp spines of the cholla
you love, the cruel blonde
spirit of the Mohave blossoming

in the spring twilights
of much earlier ages
Off at this distance I'm safe

to conjure the danger
you undergo daily, chin outthrust
eyelid lowered against the storm

that takes in an inkling whole ranches down
with the women the men and the children
the horses and cattle

—that much, flash-flood, lightning
all that had been done right, gone to hell
all crimes washed down the gulch

of independence, lost horse trail
Well, this was your country, Malinche,
and is, where you choose to speak

4.
Every drought-resistant plant has its own story
each had to learn to live
with less and less water, each would have loved

to laze in long soft rains, in the quiet drip
after the thunderstorm
each could do without deprivation

but where drought is the epic then there must be some
who persist, not by species-betrayal
but by changing themselves

minutely, by a constant study
of the price of continuity
a steady bargain with the way things are

5.
Then there were those, white-skinned
riding on camels
fast under scorching skies

their lives a tome of meaning
holding all this in fief:
star-dragged heavens, embroidered saddle-bags
coffee boiled up in slim urns
the salt, the oil, the roads
linking Europe with Asia
Crusaders, Legionnaires
desert-rats of empire
sucking the kid's bones, drunk with meaning
fucking the Arab, killing the Jew

6.
Deutsches Blut, Ahmad the Arab
tells Arnold the Jew
tapping the blue
veins of his own brown wrist
in his own walled garden
spread with figured carpets
summer, starlight, 1925
Was it the Crusader line?
Did they think it made them brothers?
Arnold the Jew my father
told me the story, showed me
his photograph of Ahmad: *Deutsches Blut*

7.
Then there were those, black-robed
on horseback, tracing the great plateaus
cut by arroyos, cleft by ravines
facing Sierra San Pedro San Mártir
a fixed bar welding Baja California
to the mainland north:
a land the most unfortunate

ungrateful and miserable of this world
Padre Miguel Venegas wrote
yet they ordered the missions raised
from fragile ramadas
the thin stream drawn from the watering-hole
into gardens of fig, palm, sugarcane
tried to will what cannot be willed
killed many in the trying:
unpacked smallpox, measles, typhus
from the chests with the linens and chalices
packed the sufferers in plague-ridden rooms
baptized in one village walk
all the children, who then died.
(San Ignacio!   Soledad!)
There were those: convinced the material
was base, the humanity less
—Out of what can I bring forth a Christian soul?
For these, naked and dark
I come to do the work of Cross and Crown?
winning hearts and minds
peeling the prickly pear
and dousing it in wine

8.
What would it mean to think
you are part of a generation
that simply must pass on?
What would it mean to live
in the desert, try to live
a human life, something
to hand on to the children
to take up to the Land?
What would it mean to think
you were born in chains and only time,

nothing you can do
could redeem the slavery
you were born into?

9.
Out of a knot of deadwood
on ghostly grey-green stems
the nightblooming cereus opens
On a still night, under Ursa Major
the tallest saguaro cracks with cold
The eaters of herbs are eaten
the carnivores' bones fall down
and scavengers pick them clean
This is not for us, or if it is
with whom, and where, is the covenant?

10.
When it all stands clear you come to love
the place you are:
the bundle of bare sticks soaked
with resin
always, and never, a bush on fire
the blue sky without tale or text
and without meaning
the great swing of the horizontal circle
Miriam, Aaron, Moses
are somewhere else, marching
You learn to live without prophets
without legends
to live just where you are
your burning bush, your seven-branched candlestick
the ocotillo in bloom

11.

What's sacred is nameless
moves in the eyeflash
holds still in the circle
of the great arid basin
once watered and fertile
probes outward through twigbark
a green ghost inhabiting
dormant stick, abstract thorn
What's sacred is singular:
out of this dry fork, this
wreck of perspective
what's sacred tries itself
one more time

1987–1988

DELTA

If you have taken this rubble for my past
raking through it for fragments you could sell
know that I long ago moved on
deeper into the heart of the matter

If you think you can grasp me, think again:
my story flows in more than one direction
a delta springing from the riverbed
with its five fingers spread

1987

It's June and summer's height
the longest bridge of light
leaps from all the rivets
of the sky
Yet it's of earth
and nowhere else I have to speak
Only on earth has this light taken on
these swivelled meanings, only on this earth
where we are dying befouled, gritting our teeth
losing our guiding stars
                          has this light
found an alphabet   a mouth

1987

FOR AN ALBUM

Our story isn't a file of photographs
faces laughing under green leaves
or snowlit doorways, on the verge of driving
away, our story is not about women
victoriously perched on the one
sunny day of the conference,
nor lovers displaying love:

Our story is of moments
when even slow motion moved too fast
for the shutter of the camera:
words that blew our lives apart, like so,
eyes that cut and caught each other,
mime of the operating room
where gas and knives quote each other
moments before the telephone
starts ringing: our story is
how still we stood,
how fast.

1987

DREAMWOOD

In the old, scratched, cheap wood of the typing stand
there is a landscape, veined, which only a child can see
or the child's older self,
a woman dreaming when she should be typing
the last report of the day.   If this were a map,
she thinks, a map laid down to memorize
because she might be walking it, it shows
ridge upon ridge fading into hazed desert,
here and there a sign of aquifers
and one possible watering-hole.   If this were a map
it would be the map of the last age of her life,
not a map of choices but a map of variations
on the one great choice. It would be the map by which
she could see the end of touristic choices,
of distances blued and purpled by romance,
by which she would recognize that poetry
isn't revolution but a way of knowing
why it must come.   If this cheap, massproduced
wooden stand from the Brooklyn Union Gas Co.,
massproduced yet durable, being here now,
is what it is yet a dream-map
so obdurate, so plain,
she thinks, the material and the dream can join
and that is the poem and that is the late report.

1987

35

WALKING DOWN THE ROAD

On a clear night in Live Oak you can see
the stars glittering low as from the deck
of a frigate.
In Live Oak without pavements you can walk
the fronts of old homesteads, past tattered palms,
original rosebushes, thick walnut trees
ghosts of the liveoak groves
the whitemen cleared.   On a night like this
the old California thickens and bends
the Baja streams out like lava-melt
we are no longer the United States
we're a lost piece of Mexico
maybe dreaming the destruction
of the Indians, reading the headlines,
how the gringos marched into Mexico City
forcing California into the hand
of Manifest Destiny, law following greed.
And the pale lies trapped in the flickering boxes
here in Live Oak tonight, they too follow.
One thing follows on another, that is time:
Carmel in its death-infested prettiness,
thousands of skeletons stacked in the *campo santo*:
the spring fouled by the pickaxe:
the flag dragged on to the moon:
the crystal goblet smashed: grains of the universe
flashing their angry tears, here in Live Oak.

1988

⳨ THE SLIDES

Three dozen squares of light-inflicted glass
lie in a quarter-century's dust
under the skylight. I can show you this:
also a sprung couch spewing
dessicated mouse-havens, a revolving bookstand
rusted on its pivot, leaning
with books of an era: *Roosevelt vs Recovery*
The Mystery & Lure of Perfume   My Brother Was Mozart
I've had this attic in mind for years
                         Now you
who keep a lookout for
places like this, make your living
off things like this: You see, the books are rotting,
sunbleached, unfashionable
the furniture neglected past waste
but the lantern-slides—their story
could be sold, they could be a prize
                          I want to see
your face when you start to sort them. You want
cloched hats of the Thirties, engagement portraits
with marcelled hair, maillots daring the waves,
my family album:
                  This is the razing of the spinal cord
by the polio virus
this, the lung-tissue kissed by the tubercle bacillus
this with the hooked shape is
the cell that leaks anemia to the next generation
Enlarged on a screen
they won't be quaint; they go on working; they still kill.

1987

37

HARPERS FERRY

Where do I get this landscape? Two river-roads
glittering at each other's throats, the Virginia mountains fading
across the gorge, the October-shortened sun, the wooden town,
rebellion sprouting encampments in the hills
and a white girl running away from home
who will have to see it all. But where do I get this, how
do I know how the light quails from the trembling
waters, autumn goes to ash from ridge to ridge
how behind the gunmetal pines the guns
are piled, the sun drops, and the watchfires burn?

I know the men's faces tremble like smoky
crevices in a cave where candle-stumps have been stuck
on ledges by fugitives. The men are dark and sometimes pale
like her, their eyes pouched or blank or squinting, all by now
are queer, outside, and out of bounds and have no membership
in any brotherhood but this: where power is handed from
the ones who can get it to the ones
who have been refused. It's a simple act,
to steal guns and hand them to the slaves. Who would have thought
        it.

Running away from home is slower than her quick feet thought
and this is not the vague and lowering North, ghostland of deeper
        snows
than she has ever pictured
but this is one exact and definite place,
a wooden village at the junction of two rivers
two trestle bridges hinged and splayed,
low houses crawling up the mountains.

Suppose she slashes her leg on a slashed pine's tooth, ties the leg
    in a kerchief
knocks on the door of a house, the first on the edge of town
has to beg water, won't tell her family name, afraid someone will
    know her family face
lies with her throbbing leg on the vined verandah where the woman
    of the house
wanted her out of there, that was clear
yet with a stern and courteous patience leaned above her
with cold tea, water from the sweetest spring, mint from the same
    source
later with rags wrung from a boiling kettle
and studying, staring eyes. Eyes ringed with watching. A peachtree
    shedding yellowy leaves
and a houseful of men who keep off. So great a family of men, and
    then this woman
who wanted her gone yet stayed by her, watched over her.
But this girl is expert in overhearing
and one word leaps off the windowpanes like the crack of dawn,
the translation of the babble of two rivers. What does this girl
with her little family quarrel, know about arsenals?
Everything she knows is wrapped up in her leg
without which she won't get past Virginia, though she's running
    north.

Whatever gave the girl the idea you could run away
from a family quarrel? Displace yourself, when nothing else
would change? It wasn't books:

it was half-overheard, a wisp of talk:
escape flight free soil
softing past her shoulder

She has never dreamed of arsenals, though
she's a good rifle-shot, taken at ten
by her brothers, hunting

and though they've climbed her over and over
leaving their wet clots in her sheets
on her new-started maidenhair

she has never reached for a gun to hold them off
for guns are the language of the strong to the weak
—How many squirrels have crashed between her sights

what vertebrae cracked at her finger's signal
what wings staggered through the boughs
whose eyes, ringed and treed, has she eyed as prey?

There is a strategy of mass flight
a strategy of arming
questions of how, of when, of where:

the arguments soak through the walls
of the houseful of men where running from home
the white girl lies in her trouble.

There are things overheard and things unworded, never sung
or pictured, things that happen silently
as the peachtree's galactic blossoms open in mist, the frost-star
hangs in the stubble, the decanter of moonlight pours its mournless
                    liquid down
steadily on the solstice fields
the cotton swells in its boll and you feel yourself engorged,
                    unnameable
you yourself feel encased and picked-open, you feel yourself
                    unenvisaged

There is no quarrel possible in this silence
You stop yourself listening for a word that will not be spoken:
                    listening instead to the overheard
fragments, phrases melting on air: *No more   Many thousand go*
And you know they are leaving as fast as they can, you whose child's
                    eye followed each face wondering
not how could they leave but when: you knew they would leave
and so could you but not with them, you were not their child, they
                    had their own children
you could leave the house where you were daughter, sister, prey
picked open and left to silence, you could leave alone

This would be my scenario of course: that the white girl understands
what I understand and more, that the leg torn in flight
had not betrayed her, had brought her to another point of struggle
that when she takes her place she is clear in mind and her anger
true with the training of her hand and eye, her leg cured on the
                    porch of history
ready for more than solitary defiance. That when the General passes
                    through
in her blazing headrag, this girl knows her for Moses, pleads to
                    stand with the others in the shortened light
accepts the scrutiny, the steel-black gaze; but Moses passes and is
                    gone to her business elsewhere
leaving the men to theirs, the girl to her own.
But who would she take as leader?
would she fade into the woods
will she die in an *indefensible position, a miscarried raid*
does she lose the family face at last
pressed into a gully above two rivers, does Shenandoah or Potomac
                    carry her

north or south, will she wake in the mining camps to stoke the
                          stoves
and sleep at night with her rifle blue and loyal under her hand
does she ever forget how they left, how they taught her leaving?

1988

ONE LIFE

A woman walking in a walker on the cliffs
recalls great bodily joys, much pain.
Nothing in her is apt to say
My heart aches, though she read those words
in a battered college text, this morning
as the sun rose. It is all too
mixed, the heart too mixed with laughter
raucousing the grief, her life
too mixed, she shakes her heavy
silvered hair at all the fixed
declarations of baggage. I should be dead and I'm alive
don't ask me how; I don't eat like I should
and still I like how the drop of vodka
hits the tongue. I was a worker and a mother,
that means a worker and a worker
but for one you don't pay union dues
or get a pension; for the other
the men ran the union, we ran the home.
It was terrible and good, we had more than half a life,
I had four lives at least, one out of marriage
when I kicked up all the dust I could
before I knew what I was doing.
One life with the girls on the line during the war,
yes, painting our legs and jitterbugging together
one life with a husband, not the worst,
one with your children, none of it just what you'd thought.
None of it what it could have been, if we'd known.
We took what we could.
But even this is a life, I'm reading a lot of books
I never read, my daughter brought home from school,
plays where you can almost hear them talking,

Romantic poets, Isaac Babel. A lot of lives
worse and better than what I knew. I'm walking again.
My heart doesn't ache; sometimes though it rages.

1988

DIVISIONS OF LABOR

The revolutions wheel, compromise, utter their statements:
a new magazine appears, mastheaded with old names,
an old magazine polishes up its act
with deconstructions of the prose of Malcolm X
The women in the back rows of politics
are still licking thread to slip into the needle's
eye, trading bones for plastic, splitting pods
for necklaces to sell to the cruise-ships
producing immaculate First Communion dresses
with flatiron and irresolute hot water
still fitting the microscopic golden wires
into the silicon chips
still teaching, watching the children
quenched in the crossfire alleys, the flashflood gullies
the kerosene flashfires
—the women whose labor remakes the world
each and every morning
                           I have seen a woman sitting
between the stove and the stars
her fingers singed from snuffing out the candles
of pure theory   Finger and thumb: both scorched:
I have felt that sacred wax blister my hand

1988

45

LIVING MEMORY

Open the book of tales you knew by heart,
begin driving the old roads again,
repeating the old sentences, which have changed
minutely from the wordings you remembered.
A full moon on the first of May
drags silver film on the Winooski River.
The villages are shut
for the night, the woods are open
and soon you arrive at a crossroads
where late, late in time you recognize
part of yourself is buried.   Call it Danville,
village of water-witches.

From here on instinct is uncompromised and clear:
the tales come crowding like the Kalevala
longing to burst from the tongue.   Under the trees
of the backroad you rumor the dark
with houses, sheds, the long barn
moored like a barge on the hillside.
Chapter and verse.   A mailbox.   A dooryard.
A drink of springwater from the kitchen tap.
An old bed, old wallpaper.   Falling asleep like a child
in the heart of the story.

Reopen the book.   A light mist soaks the page,
blunt naked buds tip the wild lilac scribbled
at the margin of the road, no one knows when.
Broken stones of drywall mark the onset
of familiar paragraphs slanting up and away
each with its own version, nothing ever
has looked the same from anywhere.

We came like others to a country of farmers—
Puritans, Catholics, Scotch Irish, Québecois:
bought a failed Yankee's empty house and barn
from a prospering Yankee,
Jews following Yankee footprints,
prey to many myths but most of all
that Nature makes us free.   That the land can save us.
Pioneer, indigenous; we were neither.

You whose stories these farms secrete,
you whose absence these fields publish,
all you whose lifelong travail
took as given this place and weather
who did what you could with the means you had—
it was pick and shovel work
done with a pair of horses, a stone boat
a strong back, and an iron bar: clearing pasture—
Your memories crouched, foreshortened in our text.
Pages torn.   New words crowding the old.

I knew a woman whose clavicle was smashed
inside a white clapboard house with an apple tree
and a row of tulips by the door.   I had a friend
with six children and a tumor like a seventh
who drove me to my driver's test and in exchange
wanted to see Goddard College, in Plainfield.   She'd heard
women without diplomas could study there.
I knew a woman who walked
straight across cut stubble in her bare feet away,
women who said, *He's a good man, never*
laid a hand to me as living proof.
A man they said fought death
to keep fire for his wife for one more winter, leave
a woodpile to outlast him.

I was left the legacy of a pile of stovewood
split by a man in the mute chains of rage.
The land he loved as landscape
could not unchain him.   There are many,
Gentile and Jew, it has not saved.   Many hearts have burst
over these rocks, in the shacks
on the failure sides of these hills.   Many guns
turned on brains already splitting
in silence.   Where are those versions?
Written-across like nineteenth-century letters
or secrets penned in vinegar, invisible
till the page is held over flame.

I was left the legacy of three sons
—as if in an old legend of three brothers
where one changes into a rufous hawk
one into a snowy owl
one into a whistling swan
and each flies to the mother's side
as she travels, bringing something she has lost,
and she sees their eyes are the eyes of her children
and speaks their names and they become her sons.
But there is no one legend and one legend only.

This month the land still leafless, out from snow
opens in all directions, the transparent woods
with sugar-house, pond, cellar-hole unscreened.
Winter and summer cover the closed roads
but for a few weeks they lie exposed,
the old nervous-system of the land.   It's the time
when history speaks in a row of crazy fence-poles
a blackened chimney, houseless, a spring
soon to be choked in second growth
a stack of rusting buckets, a rotting sledge.

It's the time when your own living
laid open between seasons
ponders clues like the *One Way* sign defaced
to *Bone Way,* the stones
of a graveyard in Vermont, a Jewish cemetery
in Birmingham, Alabama.
How you have needed these places,
as a tall gaunt woman used to need to sit
at the knees of bronze-hooded *Grief*
by Clover Adams' grave.
But you will end somewhere else, a sift of ashes
awkwardly flung by hands you have held and loved
or, nothing so individual, bones reduced
with, among, other bones, anonymous,
or wherever the Jewish dead
have to be sought in the wild grass overwhelming
the cracked stones.   Hebrew spelled in wilderness.

All we can read is life.   Death is invisible.
A yahrzeit candle belongs
to life.   The sugar skulls
eaten on graves for the Day of the Dead
belong to life.   To the living.   The Kaddish is to the living,
the Day of the Dead, for the living.   Only the living
invent these plumes, tombs, mounds, funeral ships,
living hands turn the mirrors to the walls,
tear the boughs of yew to lay on the casket,
rip the clothes of mourning.   Only the living
decide death's color: is it white or black?
The granite bulkhead
incised with names, the quilt of names, were made
by the living, for the living.
                                         I have watched
films from a Pathé camera, a picnic
in sepia, I have seen my mother

tossing an acorn into the air;
my grandfather, alone in the heart of his family;
my father, young, dark, theatrical;
myself, a six-month child.
Watching the dead we see them living
their moments, they were at play, nobody thought
they would be watched so.
                              When Selma threw
her husband's ashes into the Hudson
and they blew back on her and on us, her friends,
it was life.   Our blood raced in that gritty wind.

Such details get bunched, packed, stored
in these cellar-holes of memory
so little is needed
to call on the power, though you can't name its name:
It has its ways of coming back:
a truck going into gear on the crown of the road
the white-throat sparrow's notes
the moon in her fullness standing
right over the concrete steps the way
she stood the night they landed there.
                              From here
nothing has changed, and everything.

The scratched and treasured photograph Richard showed me
taken in '29, the year I was born:
it's the same road I saw
strewn with the Perseids one August night,
looking older, steeper than now
and rougher, yet I knew it.   Time's
power, the only just power—would you
give it away?

1988

ᛈ TURNING

I.
Deadstillness over droughtlands.
Parched, the heart of the matter.
Panic among smaller animals
used to licking water from cool stones.
Over the great farms, a burning-glass
one-eyed and wild as a jack,
the corn snatched in a single afternoon
of the one-eyed jack's impassive stare.

And in that other country
of choices made by others
that country I never chose
that country of terrible leavings and returnings
in that country whose map I carry on my palm
the forests are on fire: history is on fire.

My foot drags in the foothills of two lands;
At the turn the spirit pauses
and faces the high passes:
bloodred granite, sandstone steeped in blood.
At the turn the spirit turns,
looks back—if any follow—
squints ahead—if any lead—
What would you bring along on a trek like this?
What is bringing you along?

2.
In a time of broken hands
in a broken-promised land
something happens to the right hand

Remembering a city, it forgets
flexion, gestures that danced like flames
the lifeline buried in the fist

forgets the pedlar's trinket, fine to finger and lay forth,
the scalpel's path, the tracing of the pulse
the sprinkle of salt and rip of chicken feathers

forgets the wrist's light swivel breaking bread
the matzoh crumb
fingered to secret lips in stinking fog

forgets its own ache, lying
work-stiffened, mute
on the day most like Paradise

Becomes the handle of a club
an enemy of hands
emptied of all memories but one

When the right hand forgets its cunning, what of the other?
Shall we invent its story?
Has it simply lain in trance

disowned, written-off, unemployed?
Does it twitch now, finger and thumb,
does the prickle of memory race through?

When the right hand becomes the enemy of hands
what does the left hand make of their old collaboration?
Pick up the book, the pinch of salt, the matzoh crumb,

hand, and begin to teach.

3.
Finally, we will make change. This eyeflash,
this touch, handing the drenched flyers,
these glances back at history—

riverside where harps hang from the trees,
cracked riverbed with grounded hulks,
unhealed water to cross—

leaving superstition behind—
first our own, then others'—
that barrier, that stream

where swimming against the current will become
no metaphor: this is how you land, unpurified,
winded, shivering, on the further shore

where there are only new kinds of tasks, and old:
writing with others that open letter or brief
that might—if only—we know it happens:

no sudden revelation but the slow
turn of consciousness, while every day
climbs on the back of the days before:

no new day, only a list of days,
no task you expect to see finished, but
you can't hold back from the task.

4.
A public meeting.   I glance at a woman's face:
strong lines and soft, listening, a little on guard:
we have come separately, are sitting apart,
know each other in the room, have slept twelve years
in the same bed, attend now to the speaker.

Her subject is occupation, a promised land,
displacement, deracination, two peoples called Semites,
humiliation, force, women trying to speak with women,
the subject is how to break a mold of discourse,
how little by little minds change
but that they do change.   We two have fought
our own battles side by side, at dawn, over supper,
our changes of mind have come
with the stir of hairs, the sound of a cracked phrase:
we have depended on something.
What then?   Sex isn't enough, merely to trust   ·
each other's inarticulate sounds,
—what then?   call it mutual recognition.

5.
Whatever you are that has tracked us this far,
I never thought you were on our side,
I only thought you did not judge us.

Yet as a cell might hallucinate
the eye—intent, impassioned—
behind the lens of the microscope

so I have thought of you,
whatever you are—a mindfulness—
whatever you are: the place beyond all places,

beyond boundaries, green lines,
wire-netted walls
the place beyond documents.

Unnameable by choice.
So why am I out here, trying
to read your name in the illegible air?

—vowel washed from a stone,
solitude of no absence,
forbidden face-to-face

—trying to hang these wraiths
of syllables, breath
without echo, why?

1988

NOTES

"Sleepwalking   Next to Death": Title and opening words from "Slaap-wandelen (naast de dood)" by Chr. J. van Geel, Dutch poet and painter. For the original and my translation, see Adrienne Rich, *Necessities of Life* (New York: Norton, 1966).

"Letters in the Family, II: Yugoslavia, 1944": See *Hannah Senesh: Her Life and Diary* (New York: Schocken, 1973). Born in Budapest, 1921, Hannah Senesh became a Zionist and emigrated to Palestine at the age of eighteen; her mother and brother remained in Europe. In 1943, she joined an expedition of Jews who trained under the British to parachute behind Nazi lines in Europe and connect with the partisan underground, to rescue Jews in Hungary, Romania, and Czechoslovakia. She was arrested by the Nazis, imprisoned, tortured, and executed in November 1944. Like the other letter-writers, "Esther" is an imagined person.

See also Ruth Whitman's long poem, *The Testing of Hannah Senesh* (Detroit: Wayne State University Press, 1986).

"The Desert as Garden of Paradise," section 2: Chavela Vargas, a Mexican popular and traditional singer.

Section 3: Malintzin/La Malinche/Marina are names for an Aztec woman given as a slave to Hernán Cortés on his arrival in Mexico in 1519. Her historical reality has undergone many layerings of legend and symbolism; more recently she has become a frequent presence in Chicana feminist literature. See, for example, Norma Alarcón, "Chicana's Feminist Literature: A Revision through Malintzin," in *This Bridge Called My Back: Writings by Radical Women of Color,* ed. Gloria Anzaldúa and Cherríe Moraga (Watertown, Mass.: Persephone, 1981; distributed by Kitchen Table/Women of Color Press, P.O. Box 908, Latham, NY 12110). See also Lucha Corpi's "Marina" poems, and the author's note, in *Fireflight: Three Latin American Poets,* trans. Catherine Rodriguez-Nieto (Oakland, Calif.: Oyez Books, 1975); and Gloria Anzaldúa, *Borderlands: La Frontera: The New Mestiza* (San Francisco: Spinsters/Aunt Lute Books, 1987). Section 7: See Peter Masten Dunne, S.J., *Black Robes in Lower California*

57

(Berkeley: University of California Press, 1968); Antonine Tibeson, O.F.M., ed., *The Writings of Junípero Serra*, I (Washington, D.C.: Academy of American Franciscan History, 1955); Robert F. Heizer, ed., *The Destruction of California Indians* (Santa Barbara and Salt Lake City: Peregrine Smith, 1974); Van H. Garner, *The Broken Ring: The Destruction of the California Indians* (Tucson, Ariz.: Westernlore Press, 1982).

Sections 10, 11: Italicized phrases from John C. van Dyke, *The Desert* (1901) (Salt Lake City: Peregrine Smith, 1980).

"The Slides": Thanks to Janis Kelly for her keen eye on the medical details.

"Harpers Ferry": In 1859, the white abolitionist John Brown rented a farm near Harpers Ferry, Virginia (now West Virginia), as a base for slave insurrections. On October 16 of that year, he and his men raided and captured the federal arsenal, but found their escape blocked by local militia; the U.S. Marines then seized the arsenal. Ten of Brown's men were killed in this conflict, and Brown himself was later tried and hanged.

Harriet Tubman (1820–1913), Black antislavery activist and strategist, led more than 300 people from slavery to freedom via the Underground Railroad. She was known as "General Moses." Though in contact with John Brown, she withdrew from participation before the raid. Tubman never actually came to Harpers Ferry; her appearance in this poem is a fiction.

"Living Memory": "it was pick and shovel work . . . ," quoted from *Wally Hunt's Vermont* (Brownington, Vt.: Orleans County Historical Society, 1983).